THE CHIPPEWA

JACQUELINE DEMBAR GREENE

THE CHIPPEWA

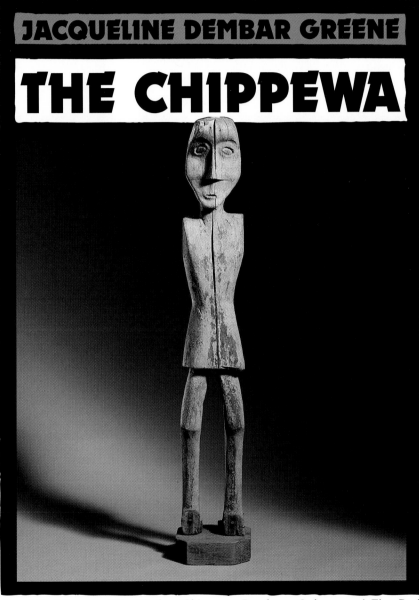

Franklin Watts   New York   Chicago   London   Sydney   A First Book

Map by Joe LeMonnier

Photographs copyright ©: cover: The Detroit Institute of Arts, Founders Society
Purchase; 3, 33: The Detroit Institute of Arts, City
of Detroit and Founders Society Purchase; 10, 13, 22, 30, 51: Ayer Collection, The
Newberry Library; 14, 21 (both), 47, 55: Rick Novitsky; 18 (top): National
Museum of American Art/Art Resource, New York; 18 (bottom): Phoebe Hearst
Museum of Anthropology, University of California at Berkeley; 25, 38: Culver
Pictures; 29: John Running; 35: National Museum of the American Indian; 41:
North Wind Picture Archives; 43, 49: Minnesota Historical Society; 44: Science
Museum of Minnesota; 57 (all): Minnesota Division of Tourism

Library of Congress Cataloging-in-Publication Data

Greene, Jacqueline Dembar.
The Chippewa / Jacqueline D. Greene.
p. cm. — (A First book)
Includes bibliographical references.
Summary: Discusses the traditional and modern way of life of the Chippewa, exam-
ining their culture, religion, and politics.
ISBN 0-531-20122-8 (lib. bdg.)—ISBN 0-531-15700-8 (pbk.)
1. Ojibwa Indians—Juvenile literature. [1. Ojibwa Indians. 2. Indians of North
America.] I. Series.
E99.C6G67 1993
977'.004972—dc20   93-18371 CIP AC

CONTENTS

This book is dedicated to the native people of the Americas, who always knew how to tread lightly on the earth.

INTRODUCTION

The native people who lived along the shores of Lake Superior called it *Kitchigami*, the giver of life. Every tree and plant, all the creatures that lived around it, and the fish that swam under its blue waves were treated with reverence, for they, too, were givers of life.

The people of Kitchigami called themselves *Anishinabe*, meaning "first man." They lived along the shores of the St. Lawrence River, then traveled west in the late 1500s looking for new hunting grounds. When they settled in the area around the Great Lakes, they were called the *Ojibwa*, meaning those who make pictographs.

The description was perfectly suited to these people who kept records of their tribe's history by paint-

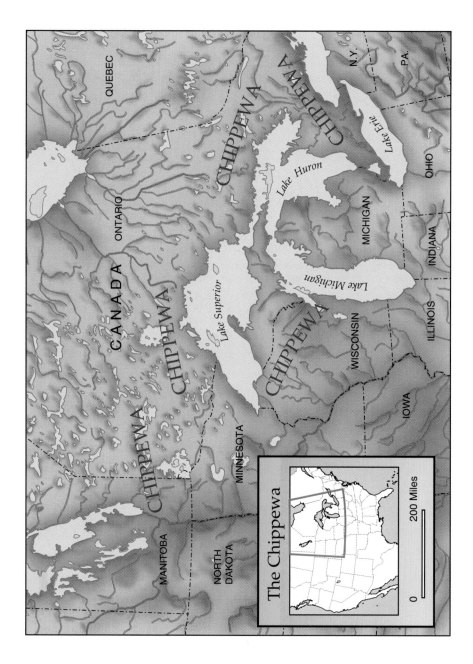

The Chippewa

200 Miles

ing pictographs on birchbark scrolls. These are believed to be the best example of written records left by any native group north of Mexico.

When the first English settlers arrived, they mispronounced the tribe's name as *Chippewa*. For the last two hundred years, it has been the official tribe name used by the United States government.

The Chippewa moved with the change of seasons to areas that provided the greatest source of food and protection. They hunted, fished, tapped maple trees for sugar, and gathered rice, berries, and nuts.

CHIPPEWA FAMILIES LIVED IN DOME-SHAPED WIGWAMS THAT WERE COVERED WITH STRIPS OF BARK. SMOKE FROM A FIRE PIT IN THE CENTER OF THE DWELLING ESCAPED THROUGH A HOLE IN THE TOP.

WIGWAMS AND BUCKSKINS

Because they moved several times during the year, the Chippewa lived in dome-shaped *wigwams* that could be built in just a few hours. Men cut young, slender ironwood trees, placed them firmly in the ground, and bent them together to form wide arches. Women tied strips of gray bark onto the frame until it was completely covered. A small hole in the top allowed smoke to escape, and there was a low doorway that could be covered with an animal hide. In winter, the wigwam was covered with an extra layer of bark.

Inside, women wove mats from bulrushes and spread them over the dirt floor. At night, the Chippewa slept under deer or bearhide blankets. In the morning, women aired them out, then rolled them up and placed them along the walls for a comfortable place to sit. A fire pit was dug in the center of the wigwam, and a fire burned all the time for light, heat, and cooking. Children collected firewood and stacked it near the entrance to the wigwam. A big sheet of birchbark over the wood kept it dry.

As many as eight family members could live comfortably in one wigwam, and two or more generations often lived together, sharing daily chores. When a family left their wigwam to travel to another area, they pulled an animal hide across the doorway and placed two long poles against it. Crossed poles across the doorway told strangers that the owners were away and that nothing inside could be diturbed.

A wigwam could be moved fairly easily from one location to another. Women rolled up the bark that covered the frame, while the men pulled the main poles from the ground. The poles were tied together to make a *travois* and many household belongings were tied onto it. This meant no new trees would be cut and a lot of time could be saved. The Chippewa might drag the travois along by hand, or harness it to their dogs to be pulled to a new site.

Clothing ➤ Most clothing was made from animal skins. After the men killed and skinned an animal, women and older girls cleaned it with a bone scraper.

LONG WOODEN POLES FROM WIGWAMS WERE SAVED WHEN A FAMILY
MOVED TO A DIFFERENT SITE. THEY WERE TIED TOGETHER TO MAKE A
TRAVOIS TO CARRY HEAVY ITEMS AND USED TO REBUILD THE WIGWAM.
THE TRAVOIS WAS USED IN MANY INDIAN CULTURES. HORSES AND DOGS
WERE USED PRIMARILY, DEPENDING ON WHICH WERE AVAILABLE.

ANIMAL SKINS WERE SCRAPED CLEAN AND
STRETCHED TO DRY ON A WOODEN FRAME.
DEERSKINS WERE USED TO MAKE MOCCASINS.

The family stretched it on a wooden frame and rubbed it with oils to make it softer and protect it from moisture. It was dried over a smoky fire. Fur was usually left on skins from buffalo, beaver, and rabbit. These hides made warm blankets or winter clothing.

Women made deerskins into clothes by sewing them with strong thread made from fibers or the sinews (long, thin tendons) of the animal. They decorated the clothing by stitching designs made with feathers, porcupine quills, shells, or beads.

Men wore buckskin shirts and tight leggings. Around their waist they wore a *breechcloth* that was often decorated with porcupine quills. Women wore deerskin dresses that were tied around the waist, or a skirt topped with a long cape. The Chippewa liked jewelry and wore shell earrings and necklaces of polished rabbit bones.

Young children wore clothes made from soft fawn skins. To keep them warm, their clothes were lined with fur from rabbits, squirrels, or beaver.

Everyone wore moccasins on their feet. They did not last long, and women were always making new pairs. Every pair had a distinctive puckered area around the toe, and moccasins were often intricately embroidered with porcupine quills and tiny beads.

There were special clothes for cold winter months. Moccasins were lined with soft rabbit fur, and Chippewa made fur sleeves to cover their arms and hands. When they went outside, they bundled up in heavy fur robes. At night, they snuggled under heavy blankets lined with rabbit fur. They slept with their clothes on and kept their feet close to the fire.

Babies were kept warm and safe on a sturdy *cradleboard* the mother carried on her back or set on the ground close to her. It was covered with buckskin, and the bottom was lined with shredded cedar bark and dry moss. A rabbitskin blanket was placed at the top, and the baby was strapped securely on with a wide strip of buckskin. A baby's arms were kept close to its sides so that its fingers could not touch. The Chippewa counted on their fingers, and they believed that if a baby's fingers touched, it was counting out the days until its death.

Chippewa all wore their hair in braids. They washed it often and rubbed it with tallow or bear grease to keep it sleek and shiny.

SEASONS OF CHANGE

Chippewa marked the passing of time according to the phases of the moon. They counted days in terms of "sleeps," and did not use the word "night." Each moon phase was named for a special event or type of weather that occurred during that month. Our month of January was called Cracking Trees Moon, February was the Deep Snow Moon, June was the Strawberry Moon, and August was the Harvest Moon.

A change of season told the Chippewa it was time to move. At the end of March, the Moon of Snowblindness, ice melted on the rivers, and a few bare patches of grass showed through the snow. The Chippewa packed their belongings onto toboggans, or the backs of their dogs, and moved into the maple

TOP, "SNOWSHOE DANCE AT FIRST SNOWFALL," A PAINTING BY
GEORGE CATLIN. BOTTOM, CHIPPEWA MADE FLAT WOODEN SLEDS
THEY CALLED "NOBUGIDABANS" TO CARRY PEOPLE AND BELONGINGS
ACROSS THE SNOW. LATER, BRITISH TRADERS MISPRONOUNCED
THE WORD AND CHANGED IT TO "TOBOGGANS."

groves. The wooden frame of the tribe's *longhouse* stood in a clearing. They went to work covering the longhouse frame with new strips of birchbark, and robes and skins were hung to divide the structure into smaller family quarters. Members of the tribe were reunited after the winter separation, and the sounds of laughter and shared stories could be heard around the camp. In the evenings, there were games, dancing, and storytelling.

Sugaring ➡ During the day, everyone worked to collect maple sap and cook it into sweet sugar. There was no ownership of trees, but each family usually tapped the same ones every year. About twenty-four trees yielded enough sap to supply one family with sugar for a year. Men used a stone axe to make a small, diagonal cut in the bark of each maple tree and then pushed in a cedar peg as a spout. They placed a birchbark bucket, called a makuk, under each spout to catch the dripping sap. The Chippewa makuks were beautiful as well as useful. Many were decorated with stenciled designs of birds, leaves, and animals cut into the outer layer of bark.

Men sharpened arrowheads and made new bows and arrows. With the spring thaw, they could hunt once again. Fresh meat and fish were smoked over a low flame so they could be dried and preserved, but there was also much feasting to celebrate the end of small winter meals that were sometimes barely enough to keep away hunger.

As the sap collected, children guarded the buckets to keep small animals away. Boys were given blunt arrows, and they would practice their hunting skills by aiming at the rabbits and squirrels that were attracted to the makuks. If by chance they killed an animal, their mother cooked it into a tasty stew.

To make fresh maple sugar, women hollowed out a large log for boiling sap while boys collected wood for a fire. As it boiled, girls stirred with a wooden paddle so it wouldn't burn. It took hours to thicken and crystallize into sugar. To test for doneness, the women would drop a bit of hot syrup into a wooden mold and set it in the snow. If it hardened into sugar, it was ready. The children were then allowed to eat some maple sugar as a reward for their help. Finally, the sugar was cooled until it was hard and ready to be stored. Maple sugar was the main flavoring in Chippewa food, and they used large quantities of it during a year.

Games ➡ By the end of maple sugaring season, the weather became warm and the ground dried. Young boys had bow and arrow shooting matches, with an older member of the tribe giving them instruction

LEFT, AS WINTER ENDS AND SPRING BEGINS, MAPLE SAP MOVES
BACK UP INTO THE TREES AND IS GATHERED FOR BOILING INTO
SYRUP AND SUGAR. RIGHT, CHIPPEWA CHILDREN STILL HELP BOIL
MAPLE SAP INTO SUGAR.

GAMES OF SKILL THAT CHALLENGED THE PLAYERS WERE A
FAVORITE PASTIME. HERE, CHIPPEWA MEN PLAY A LIVELY GAME
WITH STICKS AND BALL ON A FROZEN LAKE.

and awarding arrowheads to those who hit special targets.

In late afternoon, girls played a game called "Shinny." A goal was set up at each end of a field. Players carried bent sticks that were like today's hockey stick and tried to knock a heavy buckskin ball into the team's goal.

The day before the Chippewa left for the season, the men often organized a "Throwing Game." Women and older girls from several neighboring camps formed two teams. The game began around noontime, and spectators often placed bets on which team would win. The game was played with a *double ball*, two small balls connected with a short leather thong. It was passed down the field on long sticks toward the team's goal. If a player dropped it, the ball went to the opposing team. Teams played hard until sunset and whichever team had the most points was the winner.

Summer Camp ➤ In May, the Moon of Flowers, the Chippewa returned to their permanent homes. The longhouse was left standing, for they would return next spring to tap the maple trees again.

During the summer, groups of Chippewa lived in villages of between one hundred and three hundred people. There was no hunting during this season as it was the time of year when baby animals were born. The Chippewa did not want to accidentally kill a female or its young. They wanted the animals to increase their numbers. Fishing became the principle activity and provided the main source of food.

Everyone learned to fish, regardless of age. People used bone hooks, fiber nets, decoys, and traps. The men speared large fish such as salmon, sturgeon, and whitefish. Net traps allowed spawning fish to swim upriver to lay their eggs and to be caught only after they returned downstream. This is how the Chippewa ensured a continuous supply of fish.

Now that the soil was warmed by the sun, the people planted summer gardens. A field was prepared, and a medicine man recited prayers to the Good Spirits to help the crops grow well. A small portion of the field was set aside to grow a tobacco-like plant that was used for smoking during sacred ceremonies.

Women and children planted seeds for corn, squash, potatoes, pumpkins, and beans. Then the Chippewa prayed for the Cloud People to send rain to water the seeds.

After the corn grew tall, it was the children's job to keep birds from eating the kernels. Young girls sat on high platforms, shaking gourd rattles and flapping blankets to frighten the birds away. Boys played noisy games between the rows of corn stalks, rustling the leaves and scaring the birds.

AS THE CORN RIPENED, YOUNG GIRLS SAT ATOP WOODEN PLATFORMS
TO PREVENT BIRDS FROM EATING THE KERNELS. THEY SHOOK GOURD
RATTLES AND FLAPPED BLANKETS IN THE AIR TO FRIGHTEN THE BIRDS
AWAY. THE INSET SHOWS CHIPPEWA WOMEN MAKING ACORN CACHES
(BINS IN WHICH THE NUTS WILL BE STORED FOR FUTURE USE).

Women and children tied bark baskets around their waists and gathered berries. Cranberries grew in wet areas and were eaten fresh. Blueberries and chokeberries were dried in the sun and stored for winter use. Raspberries were boiled into a thick paste or made into pudding. Cherry twigs, wintergreen, and raspberry and spruce leaves were brewed into hot and cold drinks. Nuts and wild fruit were also added to the food supply.

Vision Quest ➡ Summer was also the season when adolescent boys and men left the village for several days alone to think, fast, and pray. Each one hoped to have a dream or a vision that would give him the power to be successful. Chippewa believed spirits sent dreams, and each was a message that revealed what might happen in the future and help guide the dreamer in his life.

When a young boy reached adolescence and was ready to seek a vision for the first time, his father came to him one morning holding a tray of charcoal. He rubbed charcoal on his son's cheeks to show others in the tribe that the boy was fasting. A father accompanied his son to a suitable location for his vision quest and would return each day, bringing water and checking his son's progress. When the young man had his dream, his father would offer food to break the fast, and they would return to the village together. A medicine man would interpret the dream's meaning. He would tell the boy about his guiding spirit, which sometimes indicated the special role the boy would fill as an adult.

As summer ended, a crier would walk through the camp early one morning and call everyone to harvest the corn. It was a community effort, with everyone working together, singing songs as they worked. Adults and tall children picked the corn while young children followed along, filling bags with the ears that fell to the ground.

Autumn Harvest ➤ In September, the Moon of Falling Leaves, the Chippewa closed their wigwams and moved to shallow lakes and streams where wild rice grew. Only small groups of families traveled to the same area they had left the year before, for there were many locations to harvest rice. A longhouse was patched with rush mats, and the families moved in.

Wild rice is a native American plant that can grow up to 10 feet (3 m) tall. The Chippewa called it *manomin*, the "good berry." Some older members of the tribe say they learned of it from other native groups. There are also some myths about how the Chippewa found wild rice. One legend tells how Winabozo, the Great Rabbit who gave the Chippewa their religion, found rice for the people during a vision quest. Chippewa sowed many rice beds, and it is now found everywhere they live.

When rice began to ripen, girls spent the day paddling canoes among the tall plants to chase away birds that would eat the grains. To keep themselves amused while they worked, they imitated animal calls, played with buckskin dolls, and chatted with each other.

As it came time to harvest the ripened grain, the girls had no time to play or visit. They paddled through the stalks constantly, chasing away birds, ducks, and geese. The girls knew they had been given a big responsibility. If they didn't protect the rice, there wouldn't be enough food for their family through the winter.

On a morning when the rice was perfectly ripe, a crier would walk through the camp, beating his drum and calling the people to begin the harvest. They set out in their canoes, with two people in each. One person would paddle up to the stalks and the second would bend them over and hit the grains with a wooden paddle until they dropped in the canoe. They returned to shore when the canoe was filled.

Children waited on shore, collected the rice in baskets, and spread it to dry in the sun. Rice was collected until only a small amount remained on the

CHIPPEWA STILL USE THEIR CANOES TO HARVEST WILD RICE
THAT GROWS ON LAKES AND STREAMS. ONE PERSON PADDLES
WHILE THE OTHER KNOCKS THE GRAINS INTO THE CANOE.

stalks. These kernels were left to fall into the water and sow new plants that would produce a fresh harvest the next year.

It might take several days to harvest, roast, thresh, and clean the rice. Finally, it was packed into

MEN HUNTED SMALL ANIMALS, SUCH AS MUSKRAT, IN THE WINTER. THEY WORE FUR-LINED SLEEVES AND MOCCASINS TO STAY WARM AND DIDN'T TRAVEL FAR FROM THEIR WIGWAMS.

makuks so each family could store their supply for several months.

Early fall was also time for hunting game so supplies of food, clothing, and tools could be restocked. Small animals such as mink, otter, beaver, muskrat, rabbit, and fox were trapped in snares. With the coming of the Snow Moon (November), men prepared to leave camp and go into the forest to hunt larger animals. About six men traveled together, and each group went to a different area so there would be enough game for all.

The hunters slept and ate without a fire so animals wouldn't be frightened away. They carried bags of dried meat and maple sugar so they would have food that didn't need to be cooked. They searched for large animals, such as moose, deer, and bear, that would provide a sufficient quantity of meat. Some blew into a birchbark cone to make a call that lured moose.

Women dried fresh meat over a low, smoky fire so it could be preserved for a long time without spoiling. They always set some aside to share during the Harvest Feast. Each family needed a good supply of meat to last through the months when it would be too cold to venture out on a hunt, or when animals were scarce, but the Chippewa did not hunt more food than they needed.

Harvest Feast ➜ On an evening after the rice had been gathered, the crier would announce that the next day would be a feast day. A special ceremony was held by the medicine men to give thanks for the bountiful harvest, and the women prepared a special community meal.

The men got up early and set the goal posts for a great game of lacrosse. Two teams of men carrying long sticks with a woven basket at the end would pass or toss a hard ball to their teammates. The game was wild and rough, with players letting out chilling yells, tripping each other, and dashing across the field with their sticks held high. The women watched and cheered as the game went on for hours. It was not over until one team scored one hundred points.

In the evening, a medicine man and members of the tribal council gathered around a blazing fire. The medicine man lit a pipe filled with sacred tobacco and raised it toward the sky, and in the direction of the four winds and the earth. He gave thanks to Father Sun and Mother Earth and blew fragrant smoke into the air so it would carry his words to the spirits. Each person in the circle took a puff of the pipe. Finally, the medicine man dropped a bit of tobacco, corn, rice, and meat on the hot coals. The ceremony ended, and it was time to eat.

The women and girls had worked all afternoon cooking food for the tribe to share. They made rice

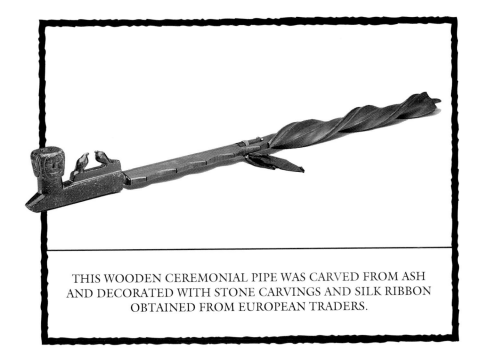

THIS WOODEN CEREMONIAL PIPE WAS CARVED FROM ASH
AND DECORATED WITH STONE CARVINGS AND SILK RIBBON
OBTAINED FROM EUROPEAN TRADERS.

and boiled ducks, roasted deer and moose meat, wild turnips boiled with maple sugar, and *pemmican,* a special treat made by pounding wild cherries together with dried meat. When the meal was finished, young children went off to sleep. Tribe elders then performed traditional dances as older children and adults watched and swayed to the rhythm of the beating drum.

Winter Camp ➦ In late fall, after the Harvest Feast, the people moved into the woods to prepare for winter. Only a few families lived in each clearing.

They shared food when it became scarce to help each other survive.

Rice was a good source of protein and was cooked many different ways. In the morning, the Chippewa ate boiled rice or rice that was cooked into hot cereal. For special celebrations, it was prepared with maple sugar, berries, meat, or fish. Sometimes it was made into soup. When traveling, roasted rice could be carried in a pouch and eaten dry.

Each family kept a clay pot of stew simmering over the fire pit. Whenever someone came in, they were offered a bowl of hot food. There were no special meal times for the Chippewa. They ate whenever they were hungry.

When the weather wasn't too stormy or cold, the men hunted. They didn't travel far from their winter wigwams so they could return each night. Sometimes they brought one or two young boys along to teach them how to hunt. Children were not considered true hunters until they killed a bear and another large animal, such as a moose or deer.

Chippewa believed that bears were sacred animals, and they held a special ceremony to honor the bear's spirit if one was killed. They felt that all animals were their brothers and were placed upon earth by the Great Spirit to help them survive. They used every part of the bear for food, clothing, or tools.

THIS VEST IS MADE FROM EUROPEAN VELVET INSTEAD OF
TRADITIONAL BUCKSKIN AND SHOWS THE ELABORATE
BEADWORK OF SKILLED CHIPPEWA WOMEN.

On snowy days, and during the long dark
evenings, men worked on animal traps and tools,
made drums and rattles, flaked arrowheads for hunting, and shaped new bows. Women kept busy weav-
ing fish nets and rush mats, and making new makuks
for maple sugar season. They cooked, sewed, and

lined moccasins and robes with fur. Whenever they had time, they embroidered designs on their family's shirts, capes, and moccasins.

In spite of the work that needed to be done each day, there was time for relaxation and games. On stormy winter days, children played in the center of the wigwam, near the warmth of the fire pit. They had tops and cornhusk dolls, round stone marbles, and toy canoes. If their father or grandfather would beat a drum for rhythm, they practiced traditional dances.

When the snow was deep and crusty, the boys went sliding on large squares of birchbark or set up targets to practice shooting. They also played a game called snow-snake. They took long sticks and flattened them on one side, then slid them across the snow to see which one would go the furthest.

Children loved snowball fights, and sometimes their parents would join in the fun. They played Blind Man's Buff, where one child was blindfolded and tried to find his playmates by listening to the sound of their voices.

To travel across the snow, the Chippewa developed snowshoes, which allowed them to walk without sinking. They also made light, flat wooden sleds to carry people or belongings great distances. These *nobugidabans* could be pulled by people or teams of dogs. The Europeans called these sleds "toboggans," a word we still use today.

Older men told folktales that showed values of courage and good behavior. They also told fairy tales that were purely for enjoyment. Sometimes they told legends about Winabozo, a godlike, cultural hero.

Every Chippewa was considered a member of one of more than twenty clans, each having an animal or bird as its *totem*, or symbol. The oldest clans were the crane, loon, bear, catfish, moose, and marten, and their members were given the privilege of speaking first at council meetings. Whenever a Chippewa traveled, he would always be welcome with a member of his clan. All members of one clan were considered relatives, even if they did not know each other.

THIS PHOTOGRAPH OF CHIPPEWA MEN SHOW THE
INFLUENCE EUROPEANS HAD ON THEIR CULTURE.
ALONG WITH TRADITIONAL HAIRSTYLES, HEADDRESSES,
AND MOCCASINS, THEY WEAR WOOLEN BLANKETS AND
CLOTH SHIRTS AND DISPLAY A METAL KNIFE AND AXE.

CULTURE AND CHANGE

The Chippewa people did not have a strong political organization, partly because they moved so frequently. The family was the center of tribal life. The most organized settlement was the summer camp, when Chippewa were in their permanent homes and the largest number of people were living in the same location.

Because the death of any person made the tribe weaker, the Chippewa were a peace-loving people. They did not have many conflicts with other tribes because there were great distances separating them.

Still, there were times when battles between tribes occurred. This happened when Chippewa tried to acquire new hunting grounds or were attacked by tribes trying to take over their territories. Sometimes, wars took place to get revenge for battle deaths that occurred in past conflicts. Wars usually occurred in summer, when traveling long distances was easiest.

Before a raid, warriors sat together and smoked their leader's colorful stone pipe. They danced around a war drum, shaking turtle shell rattles to gain courage. When it was time to leave, the wives of the warriors sang songs of farewell. Each man had a supply of bows and arrows, a long spear, a wooden club, and a thick moosehide shield to protect him from the enemy's blows. An extra pair of moccasins dangled from his belt.

The men spread out while they traveled so they could hide quickly behind a tree or bush. They were careful not to leave tracks or make noise.

When they arrived near the enemy camp, the warriors hid until the early morning hours and then rushed into the village, yelling war cries. During the battle, they took the scalps of their enemies to show their bravery. When they returned to their own village, the scalps were displayed on long poles. Later, the poles would be planted on the graves of soldiers killed in the battle.

Canoes ➤ The Chippewa perfected the art of building canoes, and today their canoes are thought to be the lightest and swiftest. Building a canoe took about

BUILDING A CANOE WAS A TASK THAT TOOK ABOUT
TWO WEEKS. MEN BUILT THE FRAME AND WOMEN SEWED
BIRCHBARK STRIPS ON THE OUTSIDE.

two weeks. A woman cleared a work site while her husband prepared strips of white cedar wood to be used for the frame. As the shell took shape, the woman cut and sewed strips of birchbark to form the outside of the canoe. Once the frame was completely covered, it was waterproofed by pouring hot spruce or pine tree *resin* over the seams. Paddles were carved from cedar wood, and each member of the family had his own.

A finished Chippewa canoe weighed between 65 and 100 pounds (29–45 kgs). It was sleek and durable, and lasted several years. A canoe could easily tip over, but the Chippewa handled them with great skill. They paddled safely through rapids and against strong currents. They always kept the paddle in the water so they could travel silently. Canoe racing was a favorite sport among both adults and young people.

Raising Children ➡ In Chippewa culture, children were especially cherished. When a baby was born, it was named after an important event that had recently taken place, an animal, or characteristic special to the child. Boys were often given names that related to successful hunting. Friends and relatives did not usually call a child by its birth name except for a special reason. Instead, people were addressed by their relationships, such as "grandfather," "aunt," "daughter," or "mother."

A child was also given a private family name that only its parents knew. This was to prevent anyone from casting an evil charm on the child. No spell could be successful without using the person's family name.

Boys were taught the ways of the forest and animals from an early age and were encouraged to be independent. When a young man killed his first large animal, there was a celebration in the village.

Girls stayed close to home and learned to cook, make clothes and baskets, and build wigwams. Young

WOMEN MADE BIRCHBARK BASKETS CALLED "MAKUKS" AND DECORATED THEM WITH STENCILED DESIGNS CUT INTO THE OUTER LAYER OF BARK.

girls helped with the harvest as soon as they were old enough to walk with their mothers.

Young men began thinking of marriage when they had become skilled hunters and could provide for a family. In the summer, when most of the tribe was together, and during the fall harvest, were the best opportunities to meet a suitable partner and spend time together. Young people were allowed to seek out their partners, and the only restriction was that two people from the same clan couldn't marry.

To propose marriage, a hunter killed a large animal and presented it to the girl's family. If the family invited him to feast with them, it showed his offer was accepted. He lived with his new wife and her family for one year. Then the couple set up a lodge of their own.

Older members of the tribe lived with their children and grandchildren, and passed on traditions, legends, and religious practices. They often were skilled at preparing herbal medicines and shared their knowledge. There was great sadness when they died.

When people died, a medicine man conducted the burial ceremony before the setting of the sun. They were dressed in their best clothes, adorned with jewelry, and placed in a shallow grave facing west, the direction for their spirit's journey to join the Dance of the Ghosts.

RATTLES WERE USED TO BEAT THE RHYTHM IN
MANY CHIPPEWA CHANTS AND DANCES. THIS ONE IS
MADE OF WOOD AND DEERSKIN, WITH DEER CLAWS
TO PROVIDE THE SOUND.

Arts ➤ Music was an essential part of Chippewa ceremonies. They shook gourd rattles and beat drums to call the spirits to come and listen. These instruments also accompanied singing, chanting, and dancing during special community feasts and celebrations. There were chants for treating the sick, during preparations for war, and at burial ceremonies. There were usually only one or two repeated words in a song, which was part of the rhythmic pattern used to express a single idea.

The flute was the only instrument that wasn't played to accompany singing. A young man would play a reed or wooden flute while he was courting. His music alerted his special woman that he was waiting nearby, and she would come to hear his serenade.

Artwork adorned most of the objects the Chippewa made. Men decorated wooden bowls with figures of people and animals. Women sewed elaborate designs on leatherwork and clothing. The Chippewa are most famous for the dental pictographs they made. Craftspeople folded thin sheets of birchbark in half and bit designs with their teeth. The lasting patterns they made were surprisingly intricate and beautiful.

Religious Beliefs ➙ Chippewa religion was based on a strong belief in spirits. *Gitchimanido*, meaning Great Spirit, was the Supreme Being. There were many lesser spirits who controlled daily life, including the amount of game, health, and the harvest. Four spirits, depicted as Thunderbirds, represented Earth's directions of north, south, east, and west. They were thought to control winds and weather.

A COVERED BIRCHBARK BASKET IS DECORATED WITH PORCUPINE QUILLS IN AN INTRICATE PATTERN. COVERED BASKETS WERE USED TO STORE RICE AND MAPLE SUGAR.

Winabozo was the spirit who was closest to the people. Before Winabozo, the tribe didn't have enough food, and were often in poor health because of their weakness. Winabozo convinced the Gitchimanido that the animals on Earth were too powerful and the people needed help. The Great Spirit then made the animals agree to allow people to use them for food. In thanks for this gift, the Chippewa would never hunt more animals than they needed.

Most ceremonies and prayers were performed daily by individuals. Gifts of tobacco were offered to the spirits when people prayed. They placed gifts of tobacco at the trunk of a tree or shrub when they collected herbs or bark and threw a bit on the water before gathering the rice harvest.

Medicine Man ➡ The Chippewa had a society of medicine men called midewiwin, meaning Grand Medicine. The *mide* learned how to cure the sick and chant healing songs. They carried medicinal herbs, barks, and roots in a special bag. In return for their help, the mide were given small gifts by the families of those they helped.

Chippewa believed medicine men had supernatural powers. Besides their healing skills, they chanted prayers to protect hunters and bring them success and also prayed for good harvests. With power gained from the Thunderbird spirits, they could bring on clouds and rain, or stop the rain and bring sunny skies. The medicine men recorded tribal history and culture on birchbark scrolls using pictographs.

Members of the Midewiwin Society trained selected young men in ritual and prayer. A student recorded what he learned on strips of birchbark, using pictographs. A young man studied many months to perfect each prayer, chant, and ritual, for it

A SOCIETY OF MEDICINE MEN CALLED "MIDEWIWIN" HAD SPECIAL
POWERS. THEY ALSO RECORDED TRIBAL HISTORY USING
PICTOGRAPHS. THIS MEDICINE LODGE WAS PHOTOGRAPHED IN
1910 ON THE WHITE EARTH RESERVATION IN MINNESOTA.

was believed that if a mide made a mistake, it might harm the patient being treated, or cause a plant to lose its healing power. A student's family gave gifts to the medicine men in return for their teaching.

For special ceremonies, a mide painted his face to indicate his rank and powers. Red face paint with a green diagonal line indicated a medicine man of the highest order in the society. Two dark lines painted upwards from the eyes indicated a mide could foretell the future.

European Contact ➤ When the Chippewa first met Europeans, they thought the rude pale-skinned men with ragged beards were dirty and greedy. They believed their own culture was superior and felt the invaders wouldn't last long in their territory. By 1659, however, the Chippewa began trading with the French, who respected the tribe's territory and customs. Some of the French married native women and joined the tribe. Chippewa traded furs for metal traps, knives, kettles, guns and gunpowder—items that made their traditional way of life easier, but eventually began to change their traditions.

The French soon built permanent homes and trading forts, to purchase pelts and to trap fur-bearing animals. Many Chippewa bands moved farther west to escape these intruders.

BY THE 1800S, CHIPPEWA HAD BECOME DEPENDENT ON AMERICAN TRADE GOODS FOR MANY OF THEIR DAILY NEEDS. FURS WERE TRADED FOR MANUFACTURED GOODS AT POSTS SUCH AS THIS ONE BUILT BY THE AMERICAN FUR COMPANY AT FOND DU LAC ON LAKE SUPERIOR.

Along with the French forts came Jesuit missions that were established to try to convert the native tribes to Christianity, although there were few conversions. The Chippewa still believed their own way of life was better than any the foreigners had to offer.

But the Chippewa eventually became dependent on manufactured trade goods. A blanket obtained for ten beaver pelts saved days of hard work skinning and treating a bear hide. A metal axe that was traded for just two beaver skins was stronger than any stone axe and did not have to be patiently chipped to a sharp point. A metal knife could be used for many daily tasks and traded for just one small pelt.

Because they needed additional animal skins for trade, Chippewa hunters began to hunt more than was needed to supply food for their families. The animal population began to decrease, and the Chippewa had to move often. Many of their traditional skills, such as making bows and arrows, preparing skins for clothing and other needs, and making pottery and baskets, were lost as ready-made items replaced them.

The Chippewa pushed farther west, taking over land from the Sioux, Fox, and Dakota tribes. By 1779, their territory stretched for a thousand miles from what is now Michigan to North Dakota. There were hundreds of Chippewa villages and camps, but instead of making the tribe stronger, it destroyed the familiar close-knit groups. The great distances between villages eliminated the traditional seasonal sites and the bonds between families and villages. The Chippewa way of life was changing drastically.

When British forces defeated the French in the late 1700s, they took over Chippewa territories on the lower Great Lakes. They increased the number of trading posts, adding to the Chippewa's dependence on European technology. After many years, the British were forced out by the Americans, who wanted to take over Chippewa lands for settlements. By 1815, the Chippewa had to trade with the Americans for the food and goods they now needed to survive.

The Chippewa continued to provide pelts, but they were offered less useful items in return, and many necessary tools were of poor quality. They stopped making clay pots, tools, and clothes. Instead, they bought wool and cotton fabric, iron kettles, needles and thread, buttons, ribbons, and beads.

For the first time the Chippewa had hunted more than they needed to feed themselves. Fur-bearing animals began to disappear, and there was a severe shortage of food. People in the villages became weak and unable to fight off diseases. Many died. The Chippewa had never been exposed to white men's illnesses before they began trading, and now, entire villages were wiped out by small pox, measles, and other contagious diseases. With fewer strong men to go on hunts, the Chippewa found themselves trapped in a cycle of hunger, illness, and death.

CHIPPEWA TODAY

After seeing the problems suffered by the Chippewa, some urged the government to establish a wilderness sanctuary where the remaining members of the tribe could live according to their traditional ways. But others, including some in the mining, lumber, and farming industries, were not as sympathetic. Throughout the 1800s, new settlers pushed the Chippewa aside. The Chippewa survived well enough when there was a plentiful supply of fish, but during the winter they did not have enough to eat. Because animals had become scarce, they also could not trap enough to collect the pelts needed for trade.

By 1854, many Chippewa were forced to sell the only thing they had left—their land. Lumber companies and developers were quick to buy up the rich forest areas, and the tribes were squeezed into smaller and smaller reservations.

To assist the Chippewa and other American Indian groups deal with their new circumstances, the U.S. government established the Bureau of Indian Affairs. Its policies forced more changes in the traditional lifestyles. The Bureau encouraged the Chippewa to become settled farmers and provided them with equipment, cattle, pigs, and seeds for planting crops. They established government schools to teach the children English, reading, writing, American history, and Christianity. Many of these changes were controversial and unwelcome.

LOGGING IS AN IMPORTANT INDUSTRY FOR THE CHIPPEWA IN MINNESOTA. HERE WE SEE A VIEW OF A SAWMILL IN GRAND PORTAGE.

With farm responsibilities tying them to one location, the seasonal way of life could not continue. Tribal festivals and the closeness of the people were being lost. The soil was not rich enough for farming, and crops were poor, meaning the people still lacked enough food. More and more Chippewa became "Americanized"—speaking English and adopting Western customs and clothes. Before the end of the nineteenth century, many began to leave the reservations for cities or took jobs in lumber camps, sawmills, and factories. About half the tribe members converted to Christianity.

After World War II, the Bureau of Indian Affairs started giving the Chippewa more independence. Older members of the tribe began teaching Chippewa culture and language in the schools. Tribal committees were established to help with housing, employment, and education. An increase in tourism provided Chippewa with traditional jobs as wilderness guides, fishermen, and craftspeople. Beadwork, moccasins, and decorated makuks were sold. The Chippewa established a summer camp for city children, where they shared their knowledge of nature.

Many young Chippewa went on to college and returned as teachers, nurses, and workers in tribal government jobs. Some light industry was begun on the reservations, providing skilled local employment.

YOUNG CHIPPEWA IN CEREMONIAL DRESS PARTICIPATE IN TRIBAL
EVENTS ON THE GRAND PORTAGE AND MILLE LACS RESERVATION. A
RENEWED INTEREST IN TRADITIONAL WAYS HAS GROWN RAPIDLY.

Some Chippewa still hunt, fish, gather berries, and make maple sugar as their ancestors did, and there is a plentiful supply of wild rice, some of which is sold.

There are now about 50,000 Chippewa, making them the third largest tribe in the United States and Canada. Only the Navajo and Sioux tribes are larger. The largest reservation, which was established in Minnesota in 1857, is called White Earth. There are nineteen other Chippewa reservations in Minnesota, North Dakota, Michigan, and Wisconsin.

In their native habitat, the Chippewa lived in harmony with their environment and did not try to change it drastically. They believed it was a privilege that nature allowed humans to survive by sustaining them. There was a spiritual connection to nature in their rituals.

Through the invasion of outside cultures, much of the traditional way of life was lost. More was lost to sickness, loss of tribal lands, the depletion of native animals, and the increased dependence on trade goods. All these things changed their relationship with the natural world. The Chippewa are now attempting to re-establish the balance between traditional culture and the realities of modern life through education and a return to native rituals and ceremonies. There is much we can learn from them to preserve our own fragile enviromental balance.

GLOSSARY

Anishinabe   A tribe of people living on the St. Lawrence River. This word means "first man," and was the early name used by the tribe later called Ojibwa or Chippewa.

Breechcloth   A length of fabric worn hanging from the waist by Chippewa men. The cloth was often embroidered with bead or quill designs.

Chippewa   The name used by English settlers to refer to the Ojibwa people.

Cradleboard   A wooden board used to hold Chippewa infants. The board could be carried on the mother's back or set upright on the ground.

Double ball   Two small balls connected by a short leather strip, used in a Chippewa women's sport called the Throwing Game.

Gitchimanido (also Kitchimanido)   This word means the "Great Spirit," the name given to the Chippewa Supreme Being in Chippewa religion.

Kitchigami   A word meaning "Giver of Life," used by the Chippewa for Lake Superior.

Longhouse   A long narrow structure used as a shared dwelling for several families.

Manomin   Chippewa word for wild rice meaning, "good berry."

Mide   A Chippewa medicine man who was skilled in healing the sick, performing religious ceremonies, and interpreting dreams.

Nobugidaban   A flat wooden sled used to carry people or belongings across the snow. This word was mispronounced by the Europeans as "toboggan."

Ojibwa (sometimes also spelled Ojibway)   Meaning "those who make pictographs," this was the name used by other tribes to designate the Anishinabe people after they migrated to the Great Lakes region.

Pemmican   A special food made by pounding dried meat and wild cherries together.

Resin   A sticky sap that the Chippewa extracted from pine and spruce trees. When heated, the sap could be poured over the frame of a canoe to seal the strips of bark and make the canoe waterproof.

Totem   An animal or bird used to identify a Chippewa's ancestry.

Travois   Two long poles used by the Chippewa to attach and carry their belongings. It could be pulled by dogs or people.

Wigwam   A dome-shaped dwelling built by Chippewa for their permanent homes. The dwelling consisted of a wooden frame covered with strips of bark.

FOR FURTHER READING

Avery, Susan and Linda Skinner. *Extraordinary American Indians*. Chicago: Childrens Press, 1992.

Beirhorst, John. *Songs of the Chippewa*. New York: Farrar, Straus, Giroux, 1974.

Osinski, Alice. *The Chippewa*. Chicago: Childrens Press, 1987.

INDEX

ABOUT THE AUTHOR

Jacqueline Dembar Greene worked as a reporter and feature writer for several years before she turned to writing for young people. Her picture book, *Butchers and Bakers, Rabbis and Kings,* was a finalist for the National Jewish Book Award. Her historical novel, *Out of Many Waters,* was named a Sydney Taylor Honor Book. She has recently completed a sequel to that novel, *One Foot Ashore.* Her most recent picture book is *What His Father Did.*

Mrs. Greene has a B.A. in French literature from the University of Connecticut and an M.A. in English literature from Central Missouri University. An avid traveler, Mrs. Greene has visited numerous Native American sites in the southwestern United States and Mexico.